Dr Freeman

The Political Catechism for 1880-1881

A Retrospect, an Outlook and a Warning

Dr Freeman

The Political Catechism for 1880-1881
A Retrospect, an Outlook and a Warning

ISBN/EAN: 9783744669634

Printed in Europe, USA, Canada, Australia, Japan

Cover: Foto ©ninafisch / pixelio.de

More available books at **www.hansebooks.com**

"Be just and fear not;
Let all the ends thou aim'st at be thy Country's,
Thy God's, and Truth's."—Shakspeare.

THE

POLITICAL CATECHISM
FOR 1880-81;

A Retrospect, an Outlook, and a Warning.

BY DOCTOR FREEMAN.

" Those that with haste will make a mighty fire
Begin it with weak straws."
Julius Cæsar.

" Suspense in news is torture : speak them out ! "
Milton.

LONDON :
KERBY & ENDEAN, 190, OXFORD STREET, W.
1880.

THE VERDICT OF THE "TIMES" ON THE GLADSTONE GOVERNMENT.

"During Mr. Gladstone's tenure of office the country has been wonderfully prosperous ; money has been forthcoming for all sorts of enterprises ; the people have lived well and spent correspondingly, and the revenue shows an elasticity marvellous in the eyes of Europe. Whoever may have been the author of the Gladstone Cabinet's Budgets, they have been framed with a sufficient knowledge of the relative productiveness of taxes, the flow of commerce, and the most abundant springs of national wealth. The Gladstone Government leaves an overflowing exchequer. There is a surplus of five millions, and a moral certainty that, if taxes to that amount were taken off, there would still be a surplus next year, owing to the regular progress of the country. Mr. Disraeli and his friends will find the house in perfect order, and a magnificent revenue to maintain it. The Gladstone Government has been a successful Government, and it has kept and left the country great and prosperous."— *Times, Feb.* 13, 1874.

What has Lord Beaconsfield done with the "MAGNIFICENT REVENUE"?

"To declare war is by our Constitution the prerogative of the Sovereign ; to grant or withhold the means of carrying it on is, by the same law, the privilege of the people through their representatives ; and by a law paramount to all constitutions—by the law of nature and necessity—**upon the people at large must fall the burdens and sufferings which are the sure attendants upon that calamity.** It seems, therefore, reasonable that they who are to suffer should be distinctly informed of the principles on which the foreign policy of the country is conducted."

C. J. FOX.

LONDON :
KERBY & ENDEAN, PRINTERS, & ., 190, OXFORD STREET, W.

DEDICATED,

WITH PROFOUND RESPECT,

TO THE CONSTITUENCIES OF GREAT BRITAIN AND IRELAND IN 1880-81,

IN THE HOPE THAT

THE FOLLOWING PAGES

WILL ENABLE THEM TO SEE THE GRADUAL DEVELOPMENT OF THEIR

CIVIL AND RELIGIOUS RIGHTS AND LIBERTIES,

AND MAY ASSIST THEIR JUDGMENT IN DETERMINING THEM TO

SUPPORT SUCH CANDIDATES AT THE NEXT ELECTION AS

WILL GIVE THEIR VOTES IN FAVOUR OF A LIBERAL, A PEACEFUL,

AN HONOURABLE POLICY IN THE GOVERNMENT OF THIS

GREAT KINGDOM,

BY THE AUTHOR.

" Of good or bad so great, of bad the sooner ;
For evil news rides post, while good news baits ;
And as some wish I see one hither speeding,
A Hebrew as I guess.

     *   *   *   *   *

" I was a fool, too rash, and quite mistaken
In what I thought to have succeeded best.

     *   *   *   *   *

" What people so expert but needs must wreck,
Embarked with such a steersman at the helm."

MILTON.

" A tempest strong is rising, Bill ;
Hark ! don't ye hear it roar now ?
Lord help 'em, how I pities them,
The Tories will be wrecked now !"

Adapted from HOOD.

" He'll no more rise,
His doom is fixed, race well nigh run—
Where is the GOOD through life he's done ?
The Echoes answer, Where ? "

FREEMAN.

INTRODUCTORY.

Q. Who are you?

A. I am a loyal citizen—and free-born.

Q. What is your interpretation of the first term?

A. Believing that limited monarchy, so long as it shall continue limited, is the best form of government for Great Britain, I desire to uphold its monarchical institutions as they existed till within the last four or five years; and so long as the reigning family shall act within the lines of the constitution, so long I will loyally and lovingly give to it my allegiance.

Q. Why do you describe yourself "free-born?"

A. The great Apostle said of himself, he was "a free-born Roman!" and claimed all the immunities and protection his citizenship secured; I, therefore, claim the privileges of my birthright, and they are—

I. *Freedom of Person*—Obeying the *just* laws of my country, the State and no official of the State dare interfere with my liberty.

II. *Freedom of Speech* — Complete liberty to express my convictions, political or religious, anywhere and everywhere, as opportunity offers, without fear and without favour.

III. *Freedom of the Press.*—For generations no
press censorship existed in Great Britain—
it has remained for Lord Beaconsfield to
curtail one of the highest privileges of
British citizenship, and I hereby enter my
solemn protest against this high-handed in-
fringement of personal and national Freedom.

*Q. In preparing the following pages, what is your
object?*

A. To educate the masses ; to spread the knowledge of simple facts ; to give subjects for reflection
to those who read ; and to dissipate the baneful
political miasma now enveloping a considerable number of the body politic.

THE
POLITICAL CATECHISM
FOR 1880-81.

" The accustomed language from the throne has been application to Parliament for advice, and a reliance on its constitutional advice and assistance. As it is the RIGHT of Parliament to give, so it is the DUTY of the Crown to ask it. But on this day no reliance is reposed in our constitutional counsels ! No advice is asked from the sober and enlightened care of Parliament ; but the crown, from itself and by itself, pursues measures that have produced the imminent perils that threaten us, the measures that have brought ruin to our doors.

"**Can the Minister of the day now presume to expect a continuance of support in this ruinous infatuation ?**" CHATHAM.

——•——

Q. Are the People of England to-day the descendants of the original possessors of the soil?

A. No ; the original occupants were barbaric and limited in number ; in England in that early age as to civilization they were as the Zulus in Zululand in this 19th century. The flint knives and arrowheads treasured in our museums evidentially proclaim their ancient condition.

Q. What became of them?

A. They were assailed by the piratical inhabitants of continental seaboards, who often made sudden forays, killing, capturing, or savagely pillaging them. Danes, Jutes, Saxons in turn amongst others, with varied success, landed and fought them, till in the end the ancient Britons were either slain, expelled into the fastnesses of the forests, or were amalgamated with their conquerors, until the common term of "England" was given to the land, and the like term of " English " to the people.*

---

* Green's History of the English People.

Q. Among the ancient English, who were their rulers?

A. They had no kings ; tribes inhabiting certain districts, as dangers increased, chose their most valorous or most discreet chiefs as leaders ; these were continually fighting, more or less, for " scientific frontiers," and not until about the 9th century after Christ did England become one country under one sovereign.

Q. When was Wales brought under English rule?

A. In 1157 Henry II. made inroads into South Wales and " rectified " his frontiers, but not till 1282 did Edward II. completely subjugate the Principality ; in 1536 it was united to England by Act of Parliament.

Q. When and how did Scotland become united to England?

A. Strife and bloodshed was the chronic state between England and Scotland for many generations, but on the death of Queen Elizabeth in 1603, James VI. of Scotland was called to the throne of England as James I., and was proclaimed King of England, Wales and Scotland in 1604. In 1707 the union of the kingdoms was effected.

Q. How fared Ireland during these ages?

A. Worse than her neighbours ; before and after the baptism of St. Patrick the Irish had their baptisms of blood ; again and again had English forces marched through and through the land, spreading destruction everywhere. History states that, whilst King John reigned over the Irish in 1210, it was not till 1800-1801 the Act of Union was passed completely bringing Ireland within the jurisdiction of the British Crown. On January 2, 1801, the first Parliament of the *United* Kingdom of Great Britain and Ireland assembled in Westminster, during the sovereignty of George III.

Q. What is the present extent of the British Dominions?

A. The subjects of the Queen, governed by her laws, inhabit Great Britain and Ireland, Canada, India, the West Indies, Australia, South Africa, Malta, Gibraltar, and many colonies of more or less note in various parts of the world.

Q. By what means has the power of England become so widely extended?

A. By Conquest; by Consent; by Colonization.

Q. Can you illustrate this statement?

A. Yes; by *Conquest*, as India. In 1591 the East India Company made its first venture; received its first Charter in 1600; by intrigue and by force of arms gradually brought this great Empire, with 200,000,000 subjects, under British dominion; the Company ceded its powers to the Crown on the 1st of September, 1858. Wales and Ireland, also, may be said to come under this designation. In 1284, on the Queen giving birth to a son in Caernarvon, to conciliate the Welsh he was proclaimed "The Prince of Wales," and was the first of a long line of Princes so named who have inherited the British throne.

II.—By *Consent*, as Scotland, which was an independent kingdom till 1707; on the death of Queen Elizabeth, James VI. of Scotland became James I. of England, and so, in 1603, the Crowns were united; the complete union of the Kingdoms being consummated in 1707.

III.—By *Colonization*, as Canada, Australia, New Zealand, Tasmania, British Columbia, and many other colonies, peopled by emigrants from the mother country, taking with them her laws, institutions, and government.

Q. The power and dominion of the kingdom being so widely extended, what is the form of government under which the people live?

A. A limited monarchy—neither absolute nor imperial.

Q. What do you mean by "absolute" or "imperial" government?

A. An absolute or imperial government is that wherein the ruling power is vested in one individual, whose will is law, or above law, whose word takes away or spares life ; who claims to hold the conscience, the liberties, the lives of his subjects in his hands, and for whom the people are supposed to exist, as is the case in Russia.

Q. Is this form of government adapted to the English race?

A. It will be well for Earl Beaconsfield and for her Majesty the Queen to remember the past, and long to hesitate ere taking further steps in this direction.

Q. What is a "limited" Monarchy?

A. A limited monarchy is that wherein the sovereign can neither legislate nor impose taxes without consent of Parliament ; usually does not venture to declare war or make peace of his own will ; is bound personally to conform to the law. If he or his advisers override the law, he or they become responsible to the nation, and are amenable to impeachment, trial, and death, if need be, for so doing.

Q. What is meant by the term "Law"?

A. This is a very comprehensive and difficult term to define ; it is a body of rules, written or unwritten, that have grown into existence with the growth and experience of ages, having for their object the common weal of every subject ; the protection of every national, inherited, or acquired right of the individual, of the family, or of the whole nationality, subject to modifications, or to abrogation, as the necessities of the people or of the times may demand.

Q. What are the classifications of the laws?

A. Divine law, or laws enjoined by natural or revealed religion ;

Civil or Municipal law, as affecting a community or country;

Canon law, as touching all matters ecclesiastical;

Common law, or law unwritten, holding its force from the practice of states, or of certain classes in the state, from age to age.

Q. What am I to understand by the term Government?

A. The possession of power to control whatever is within the province of the controller, as the pilot governs the ship with his hand upon the helm, is government in its simple meaning; but when we speak of the government of the country, we mean primarily the members of the Cabinet (so-called), commissioned by the Sovereign to control the affairs of the nation.

The English Cabinet has no legal recognition by the law; its members are never officially announced as such; it keeps no minutes of its proceedings, or even of its official meetings, no Act of Parliament has ever recognised its existence—its members usually represent the stronger political party in the House of Commons; the First Lord of the Treasury is the Premier of the Cabinet, and he may be taken from either House.

Q. Does it follow that the men forming the Cabinet are always the most competent, honourable, and worthy of credit in the realm?

A. By no means, though the exceptions are rare; able statesmanship, which grasps the movements of the hour, calculates and forecasts with precision the results of given action, controls or fascinates with foresight and skill the movements of friendly or unfriendly powers, may be wholly wanting, as is the case at present; in the place of it we may have daring speculators risking the nation's welfare by intrigues, by craft and cunning, by secret treaties, meddling and muddling with the national finances all but irremediably, making almost bankrupt the nation's reputation for integrity and honour, and giving cause in itself and in its utterances for the strong declaration of Mr. Cross, the Home Secretary, " there IS a lying spirit abroad."*

Q. Into how many parts is the Government divided?

A. Three, known as the Three Estates of the Realm : Queen, Lords, Commons.

Q. What share has each in governing?

A. The Cabinet or the Commons initiate the bills proposed to become law ; the Lords veto or sanction them ; the Crown accepts or rejects. If accepted, the Queen appends her signature, and from that moment the bill becomes law, but not till then ; if she refuse to sign, the bill ceases to be of force. The Lords also have power to introduce bills first into their House ; if accepted, they are submitted to the Commons, which deal with them in the same way as if first introduced into their own House.

Q. Is it essential to the validity of a proposed law that the Three Estates agree?

A. Yes ; the Commons can make no law of itself, neither can the Lords, nor the both together : the consent of the Monarch is absolutely necessary. But neither can the Monarch ; by himself he is as powerless as they, and herein lies the safety of the Constitution ; each by itself is an ever-wakeful check upon the lust for power of the other two.

Q. With whom lies the Power of the Sword?

A. With the Monarch ; this power it was sup-posed, *until recently*, the Monarch would never venture to exercise without the consent of the House of Commons.

Q. Why should not the Monarch declare war of his own will?

A. Because the lust for power is so great monarchs would ever be embroiling their subjects in war, and

---

* Hansard's Debates, vol. 237.

the calamities and scourges it entails would never be absent from the land.

Q. As the Monarch can declare war if he will, what wholesome check have the people to prevent it?

A. The Power of the Purse, that is, the power to grant or withhold payment of the costs. Unnecessary wars will not be waged if the people refuse to pay for them, and English monarchs are kept in check by this great safeguard.

Q. In what year did Parliament first assemble?

A. In 1205 King John issued to his Barons the first summons by writ to assemble for counsel on the state of the realm; in 1258 the then Parliament is said to have consisted of twelve persons only; in 1265 the House of Commons as such first took permanent form, and was composed of knights, citizens, and burgesses as now.

Q. In the early days of Parliamentary government was the power of the Commons great?

A. No; more frequently it was the creature of the reigning sovereign, and a ready tool for his purposes; in spite of this it gradually assumed power, became more and more the House of the people, and resisted encroachments of reigning sovereigns, until it has become the chief power in the kingdom.

Q. In what spirit have the institutions of the country been enacted?

A. In the spirit of Freedom; not all at once, but step by step the English Constitution has been formed; *all subjects are now equal before the law*, are at liberty to go whither, when, and how they will, and, having broken no law, the State dares not interfere with the liberty of the subject.

Freedom of Speech is the nation's birthright; if this freedom be wickedly abused against individuals, or against the State, laws exist sufficiently powerful to meet such cases.

Religious Toleration, or the right of every man to choose for himself his creed and his church, is the inheritance of every Englishman. This has been confirmed by the Abolition of the Test and Corporation Acts, by the Roman Catholic Emancipation Act, and by the Removal of the Disabilities of the Jews.

A Free Press is national property, or at least so we believed till recently. Till of late, war correspondents were the necessary accompaniment of every military operation. On this point we were examples to the world, and the immense benefits they conferred by their truthfulness is matter of history. To Lord Beaconsfield we are indebted for the reversal of this policy. He has curtailed the liberty of the press ; permits no news to be given without sanction of the military authorities, who delay it at pleasure or drop it by the way, until nobody believes the telegrams or accepts them as probably true. The Indian press regulations are an Imperial menace to the liberty of the press.

Q. Was this gagging of the Indian press an act of the Indian Council, or an act of Lord Beaconsfield's Government ?

A. Of Lord Beaconsfield's Government—the Imperial order emanating from his Cabinet passed through the War Office to India, to be enforced without the power of the Viceroy to alter a single article of the instructions so sent ; this order has not been submitted to Parliament.

Q. To what is the nation mainly indebted for securing its rights and liberties ?

A. To *Magna Charta*, the Great Charter or written record of the People's Rights and Liberties, granted by King John on June 15, 1215, the Barons of that day compelling the King to sign it.

To the *Bill of Rights*, compulsorily signed by King Charles I. on June 26, 1628, the " Second Great

Charter of the Liberties of England. By ratifying this law he bound himself never again to raise money without the Consent of the Houses, never again to imprison any person except in due course of law, and never again to subject the people to the jurisdiction of Courts Martial," * and the ink of his signature was scarcely dry ere he began to use most strenuous endeavours to upset the whole contents of the Bill he solemnly pledged himself to enforce.

To *the power of Public Opinion*—To-day it is dangerous to attempt to pass laws infringing upon the liberty of the subject, of the press, or of speech; public opinion is the power of the people giving strength to the throne, and is stronger than the throne itself. If the Government of Lord Beaconsfield desire to foster and augment an adverse spirit among the people, they need march only a very little further on the road in which they now are, and I will not presume to answer for the consequences.

Q. Have attempts been made to Curtail the Freedom of the People?

A. Yes, many, but success was short-lived.

Q. Can you name any special instances?

A. Yes: Charles I., having solemnly and publicly granted the Petition of Right, exercised his utmost ingenuity to render it abortive; persevering in his attempts to rule as an *absolute* monarch without a parliament, he was arrested, arraigned, and judicially condemned to death for his high crimes and misdemeanours against the liberties of the people.

By Charles II, on many occasions, but the people at last extorted from him the Habeas Corpus Act on the 26th of May, 1679. By this Act, any person imprisoned on any charge by any Court, or by the Crown, has the right to claim a writ of Habeas

* Macaulay's History of England.

Corpus compelling the authorities to produce him at the bar of the Court of Queen's Bench, or of the Court of Common Pleas, and the said Court before which he is brought must determine on the justice or injustice of the commitment.

By James II. so repeatedly, and with such ungovernable ferocity, that he was driven from the throne, fled the country, and died in exile. And from the period of his flight succeeding monarchs have governed more or less in accordance with the spirit of the Constitution. Under the Beaconsfield *régime* there is a strong tendency developing itself towards the monarch reigning as the representative of an Imperial dynasty, and not as the Constitutional monarch of a free people.

Q. Do the members of the Houses of Parliament agree in their principles of government?

A. No; they are divided mainly into two parties— Whigs (or Liberals) and Tories (Conservatives). Two other terms are also descriptive of members of the House : " Liberal-Conservatives" and " Radicals."

Q. When were the names Whig and Tory first used politically?

A. In the reign of Charles II. At first "nicknames" given in scorn, they were soon proudly assumed as badges by persons so designated ; they are now the distinguishing terms by which the two great parties in the State are known.

Q. Define the term " Whig."

A. When first used it denoted a man whose principles led him to oppose the licentious extravagance of the Court, and to demand that Protestant Nonconformists should be treated with justice.

Q. Define the term " Tory."

A. This term was first applied to Englishmen who were ready to place a Roman Catholic Prince upon the throne contrary to law.

Q. What is a Tory to-day ?

A. He is one who believes in the divine hereditary right of kings, in passive obedience, royal prerogative, lineal succession, &c. James I. said, " As it was blasphemy to question what the Almighty could do of His power, so it was sedition to inquire what a king could do by virtue of his prerogative," * but the royal prerogative is now virtually subject to Parliament, unless an audacious minister chooses to override the Parliament and to stretch the royal prerogative at his pleasure in spite of the will of the Commons. The policy of the Tory is to keep *all* power, of *any kind*, as much as possible *out of the hands of the people*, and to maintain Church and State under any circumstances, without regard to efficiency or economy of administration in either the one or the other.

Q. What is a Whig to-day ?

A. He is the opposite of the Tory. Equally loyal to Crown and Constitution, his efforts are given to increase the power of the people, for whom governments exist; to enact laws having for their object the general good, and he labours to give to every subject active interest in the security of the State, and to keep the costs of Government free from wasteful extravagance.

Q. What is a " Liberal-Conservative ? "

A. He is a man who believes in the gullibility of the British public—calling himself a Liberal-Conservative, he strives to convince Liberal electors he is as good a Liberal as he who is nothing but a Liberal ; often says, "there is not a pin to choose between us;" that he, in fact, belongs to both parties ; but, tested by facts, the term is found to be a wretched sham. All Liberal-Conservatives sit on the Tory side of the House, and so sitting are safely relied upon for their votes, no matter how " Liberal " (?) their convictions may be, nor how

* Macaulay's History of England.

strongly they condemn the votes given—they form part of a solid block that moves forward or backward as " whipped " by the Tory whip.

Q. What does the term " Radical" mean ?

A. A Radical mostly lives in advance of his age ; for him the world does not move quickly enough. He looks ahead and sees in the future governmental and national reforms he would prefer having to-day, but cannot ; he therefore works in favour of that policy which will the more readily bring about what he believes to be for the good of his country ; and it so happens that Radicals have often proved the pioneers of progress. What a few such men in one age have deemed the greatest good, and for which they strove amid obloquy and scorn, the men of a succeeding generation have given ungrudgingly and with the most beneficial results.

Q. Can you illustrate the way in which Tories and Whigs have carried their principles into practice?

A. Nothing more easy. For example, Charles I., in his long career of oppression with and without Parliament, in his wholesale imprisonment of his subjects, in his tyrannical proceedings against their rights and liberties, resulting finally in the loss of his Crown and his life, was supported throughout by the Cavaliers—the Tories of that day—they being the avowed upholders of Church and State at any cost.

Under his reign the nation had sunk from the proud position she occupied in the days of Henry VIII. and Queen Elizabeth to that of a third or fourth-rate state ;—Cromwell and his co-workers, the Whigs of that day, raised her again to the front rank among nations: in *every step* of his progress *he was opposed by the Tories.*

The Restoration of Charles II. was their work. This King was the most dissolute and corrupt that ever sat on the English throne. Accepting the Crown as a Protestant, swearing to maintain Protestantism, he died a Roman Catholic, refusing to receive the Sacrament of the Holy Communion in the English Church, and proved himself a renegade to his oath.

The acceptance of the Duke of York as King James II. was the work of the Tories. He was an avowed and well-known Roman Catholic ; a bill to secure his exclusion from succeeding to the throne on the death of his brother, Charles II., was carried in the House of Commons by a large majority, but the King evaded it. Though *a bigoted Roman Catholic, he hesitated not to take the oath of supremacy as a Protestant*, and immediately afterwards introduced Roman Catholics into his household.

His tyrannical and despotic proceedings were supported by the Tories—in his reign the " bloody assizes " were held by Judge Jeffreys, who was the willing and bloodthirsty tool of the Popish King, and a Tory.

Q. Are there any later illustrations of the tendency of Toryism?

A. Many—from that day every measure for enlarging the privileges of the people has been strenuously opposed by them—the Abolition of the Slave Trade ; Removal of the Test and Corporation Acts ; Roman Catholic Emancipation ; Municipal and Parliamentary Reform ; Repeal of the Corn Laws; Free Trade and the Abolition of Protective Duties—in fact, every measure tending to promote the welfare of the people has met with determined opposition from the Tories; but they are always ready to be "educated" by their leaders to sacrifice all former professed principles at the shrine of place and power, to pass Reform Bills, or any Bill whatsoever that will have the effect of keeping them in office.

Q. What is the policy of the Whigs or Liberals?

A. On the side of the people, as the guardians of their rights and liberties, they or their policy

obtained Magna Charta ; they resisted the encroachments of Charles I. ; won the " Petition of Right,"
and at last, in self-defence, seized the throne ; they
upheld Cromwell in his Protectorate, causing the name
of Englishman to be again respected and feared in
every quarter of the globe ; they resisted the vile and
extravagant corruptions of the Court of Charles II.,
and secured the Habeas Corpus Act ; driven to
desperation by James II., they expelled him from
the throne he occupied only to defile, and placed
William of Orange thereupon ; established the Protestant Succession—and from that day the constitution
that now exists was consolidated mainly through the
legislative improvements introduced and carried out
by them.

Q. Can you give later developments of Whig principles?

A. Having seen the great measures they resolutely
placed upon the Statute-book on behalf of the people,
recent events show how thoroughly they are the best
promoters of all that is for the good of the community
—amongst other measures they Abolished the Taxes
on Knowledge ; Removed the Disabilities of the Jews ;
and when, in 1868, they endeavoured to pass a
moderate Reform Bill, Mr Disraeli denounced them,
with great vehemence, as he said, " for their extreme
democratic measure,"* and succeeded in overthrowing
it ; this led to his being called to office as Tory
Premier.   He then introduced a bill far more
democratic than that he overthrew—greatly alarming
his Tory followers—but so crude and unstatesman-
like were its details that not a single particle of
his bill as introduced was passed but the word
" whereas ; "   the House evolved from itself the
Reform Bill (so-called) of the Tory Government, Mr
Disraeli succeeding in " educating " his followers to
swallow the bolus they so much detested, but swallowed
it in order to retain office.

Further, they Disestablished the Irish Church, the

---

* Hansard's Parliamentary Reports.

standing grievance of Ireland; passed the Irish Ten-
ant Right bill; brought into existence the Educational
system now in operation, with future advantage
to the poor; abolished Purchase in the Army, so that
now capacity has the chance of success it never before
possessed; passed the Ballot act, and many other
great and important laws aiming at social and domestic
happiness.

*Q. As the policy of Liberalism clearly has ever been
on the side of beneficent progress, I would ask if this
has not resulted in increased taxation and enlarged
expenditure?*

A. It is a singular fact, a fact that cannot be dis-
proved, that when a Tory ministry is in office taxation
increases, and the spending powers of a Tory government rapidly extend. Take any Tory administration
for the last hundred years, and *this is the inevitable
result.* Whig ministries have always striven for
economy, for retrenchment of the costs of Government, for remittance of taxation, for lessening the
burdens of the people, so that the legislative results
of Liberalism are always economical and beneficial to
the nation and to every individual in the nation.

*Q. Is not this a prejudiced statement? Can you
prove it?*

A. We need not travel far in search of proof. The
experience of the last hundred years is amply illustrated by the present Tory administration. In the
following figures the reader will see for himself with
what tremendous power they emphasize the blessings
of Liberal Government over Tory administration, and
they eloquently give their verdict in favour of the
former:

RETURN OF THE INCOME AND EXPENDITURE OF GREAT BRITAIN FROM JANUARY 1, 1869, TO DECEMBER 31, 1879, A PERIOD OF ELEVEN YEARS.

MR. GLADSTONE'S ADMINISTRATION.

Years.	Income.	Expenditure.	Surplus.	Deficit.	Years.
1869	72,605,823	75,586,022	——	2,980,199*	1869
1870	75,674,196	69,152,342	6,521,854	——	1870
1871	70,358,743	69,779,314	579,429	——	1871
1872	75,276,198	71,946,618	3,329,580	——	1872
1873	77,123,469	71,102,896	6,020,573†	——	1873

Totals for the 5 years of Mr. Gladstone's Government. £371,038,429 £357,567,192 £16,451,436 £2,980,199* 5 years

EARL BEACONSFIELD'S ADMINISTRATION.

Years.	Income.	Expenditure.	Surplus of Income over Expenditure.	Excess of Expenditure over Income.	Years.
1874	£76,788,168	£77,044,852	none	£256,684	1874
1875	75,000,592	75,004,184	none	3,592	1875
1876	77,078,405	80,947,630	none	3,869,225	1876
1877	78,562,111	79,108,429	none	546,318	1877
1878	80,189,250	83,292,584	none	3,103,334	1878
1879	83,098,735	85,857,789	none	2,759,054	1879

Totals for 6 years of Earl Beaconsfield's Government. £470,717,261 £481,255,468 none £10,538,207 { 6 years of Tory rule.

In order to compare an equal period of the two Administrations, we will deduct from the foregoing return of Earl Beaconsfield's six years the year 1874, so that we shall then have five complete years of each Administration. Thus, deduct—

1874 £76,788,168 £77,044,852 ... none ... £256,684

Totals for 5 years of Earl Beaconsfield's Government, ending Dec. 31, 1879. £393,929,093 £404,210,616 no surplus £10,281,523 { 5 years of Tory rule.

Totals of 5 years of Mr. Gladstone's Government. £371,038,429 £357,567,192 £16,451,436

Results in favour of Liberal Government. £22,890,664 £46,643,424 £16,451,436 { A large Surplus made every year.

* 1869.—Grant made of £3,600,000 to cover the costs of the Abyssinian war. This war was declared in 1868 by Mr. Disraeli, who asked for the sum of £5,000,000 as ample to cover the costs, but the extravagance was found to have been so great that this further sum was rendered necessary to wipe out the liabilities incurred.

† This left a legacy to Earl Beaconsfield on taking office in February, 1874, of about £6,000,000, and this, after paying in this year nearly 3½ millions to cover the Alabama indemnity, the agreement to submit the American claims to arbitration and to abide by its decision having been made in 1868 by Earl Beaconsfield, then Mr. Disraeli; and the present Chancellor of the Exchequer was one of the representatives of Great Britain before the Arbitration Court.

Thus the present Tory Government has received
during the last 5 years a larger income than that
received in the 5 years of Mr. Gladstone's administration of no less a sum than £22,890,664
In the 5 years its expenditure has exceeded 5 years
of Mr. Gladstone's Government by the enormous
sum of £46,643,424
These then are the facts :—The 5 years of Liberal Government,
from Jan. 1, 1869 to Dec. 31, 1873, cost £357,567,192 ; the
income of the 5 years exceeding the expenditure by
£16,451,436, and that after paying the Alabama award and
the supplemental costs of the Abyssinian war, the two together making about £7,000,000, and having further reduced
the taxation of the country to a very large extent. The last
5 years of Tory Government cost £404,210,616, an excess
over Mr Gladstone's expenditure of £46,643,424.
The present Tory Government has drawn by taxation from the pockets of the people in the 5
years ending Dec. 31 last more than was drawn
by the Liberal Government in 5 years the large
sum of £22,890,664
In addition to this its expenditure has exceeded its
very largely increased income by the sum of ... 10,281,523
Add to this the legacy left to the Tory Government
by Mr. Gladstone on leaving office in Feb., 1874,
of his surplus of 6,000,000
_____

And we thus have in 5 years the enormous penalty
laid upon the nation for Tory Government instead
of Liberal Government, in **excess of the usual
costs of Government of** £39,172,187
The Tory Expenditure for the last five years has exceeded the
5 years of Mr. Gladstone's Administration by the sum of
£46,643,424, or an average of additional cost for Tory Government over Liberal Government of

NEARLY TEN MILLIONS A YEAR !!

Electors of England! how do YOU like paying an increased
expenditure of Ten Millions a year for Tory rule in preference
to Liberal rule ?

Electors of Wales, of Scotland, of Ireland! how do YOU like
paying an increased expenditure of Ten Millions a year for Tory
rule in preference to Liberal rule ?

Is it not time to say as was said by a sturdy and noble Englishman
of a former age, " Remove this bauble! Remove this bauble ?"

On Mr. Gladstone's retirement from office in 1874 the country was in great prosperity; its wealth was increasing by "leaps and bounds;" at peace with all the world and holding amicable relations with all; the income largely exceeding the expenditure; legislative efforts developing such reforms as promoted the good of the nation at home, and whilst thus pursuing a thoroughly domestic policy, he was wisely husbanding the national resources so that, if driven to speak in the councils of Europe, it should be with energy and power as the voice of the WHOLE nation. But, whilst thus wisely governing, the Liberal administration was, with equal wisdom, taking no adverse step to force on great European wars; was not playing into the hands of Russia in the East, nor saddling the nation with responsibilities likely some day to test its powers to bear, and the costs of government for all charges on his leaving office were covered in round numbers by £71,000,000 a year.

Q. Now what is the result of the Beaconsfield or Tory policy?

A. The nation is crying out in many parts from distress—trade depressed everywhere; the burdens of the people increasing every day; little domestic legislation even attempted; added to this, at a time when it can ill be borne, we have enormously increased expenditure of public funds; great marching of armies in various countries — a naval and military cost increased from £24,000,000 to over £32,000,000 a year; thousands and tens of thousands of human beings—our own sons and the children of Africa and India—butchered wholesale in war, or dying from the effects of war; rapine, ravage, burnings, hangings on such a scale as to sully the fair reputation of England for all time to come; and what has resulted from the course the Tory Government has taken? and taken at a cost in round numbers of over £85,000,000 a year!

Have we endeavoured to emancipate Christian communities from the tyrannical and oppressive yoke of Turkish misgovernment? No! we aided the Turks in their oppressions.

Have we preserved the integrity of the Turkish Empire? No!

Have we subdued and put an end to discontent and incipient rebellion in South Africa? No! On the contrary, South Africa threatens more to-day than it did three months since.

Have we subdued and brought under our control the Afghans, or obtained any indication that they will submit to our government? No! Far otherwise. Driven from one stronghold they decamp and rise up in another in still greater numbers, so that none can tell when again the state of war in Afghanistan will cease.

Have we obtained a single ally in Europe to unite with us in the course we have taken? Not one! They look upon the proceedings of the government amazed; it is a subject of humorous remark amongst the Continental powers.

Have we obtained such a holdfast on Turkey, or so bound her to us by gratitude for our support, that she will readily comply with any expressed wish we may present to her? Let the action of our Ambassador in obtaining the papers of a simple citizen and the deliverance of a Mussulman subject from death, for no crime, speak the answer. He was compelled to solicit the German representatives to unite with him in his demands ere they were granted; and the very official whom Sir H. Layard sought to expel is raised to greater dignity. Surely the proof is given on every hand that the Beaconsfield policy is an utter failure in every part of the world in which it has been put into action.

Q. Who are the representative men of the Liberal Party?

A. The Right Honourables William Ewart Gladstone, John Bright, Earl Granville, The Marquis of Hartington.

Q. Who is Mr. Gladstone?

A. He is the fourth son of the late Sir John Gladstone, a merchant of Liverpool ; he was born in 1809; was a double-first-class-man at Oxford in 1831 ; sat for Newark from 1832 to 1845 ; a Lord of the Treasury in 1834-5 ; Under Secretary for the Colonies in 1835 ; Master of the Mint and Vice-President of the Board of Trade, 1841-43 ; President of the Board, 1843-1845 ; Colonial Secretary, 1845-46 ; represented the University of Oxford, 1847-1865 ; Hon. D.C.L., 1848 ; Chancellor of the Exchequer, 1852-55 ; again, 1859-66 ; Lord High Commissioner Extraordinary of the Ionian Islands, 1859 ; Lord Rector of the University of Edinburgh, 1859-65 ; Member for South Lancashire, 1865; for Greenwich, 1874 ; succeeded to the Leadership of the Liberals on the death of Lord Palmerston, and was the Liberal Premier from Dec. 9th, 1868, to Feb. 17th, 1874.

Q. What opinion is generally entertained of him?

A. That he is a man of transcendent abilities ; " Touches no subject but he adorns it " (Earl Harrowby's speech—a Tory!) is the first financier of the age ; thoroughly honest in his principles and motives ; *has never been known to sacrifice principles for place, but has more than once sacrificed place to maintain his principles;* labours assiduously for the benefit of the masses of his fellow-countrymen, and strives to reduce that *wasteful national expenditure for which the Tories are celebrated;* is of world-wide reputation—the first orator of the age, and one of the most honest, conscientious, and fearless men to be found in the House of Commons or in the Kingdom —an honour to his family, to his constituency, to his country, and to the manhood of the world.

Q. How has he been described by one of the highest legal authorities of the day?

A. Lord Selborne said of him : " I have known Mr. Gladstone long, and I think, in point of conscientiousness, in point of earnestness, in point of vehement burning zeal against abuses of every kind, in point of disinterestedness, and in point of sympathy with the people at large, *I have never known any statesman who was his equal*, much less his superior."

Q. Who is Mr. John Bright?

A. He was born in 1811 ; is a member of the Society of Friends ; a partner in the firms of John Bright and Brothers, cotton spinners and manufacturers, Rochdale ; and Bright and Co., carpet manufacturers, Rochdale and Manchester. His first appearance in public was as an advocate of Reform in 1831-32 ; in 1839 he joined the Anti-Corn-Law League, and was one of its earliest members. In April, 1843, he contested Durham, and lost the seat, but in the July following he was elected member for that city, which he represented till 1847, when he was returned for Manchester, which he represented till 1857 ; the state of his health preventing his appearance at the election which took place in the early part of 1857, he was defeated, but in the August of the same year he was chosen Member for Birmingham, which constituency he still represents ; was President of the Board of Trade in Mr. Gladstone's Cabinet in 1868.

Q. What can you say of Mr. Bright?

A. I adopt the language of a late Mayor of Birmingham (a Tory) who thus spoke of him at a banquet :—" In our senior member, Mr. Bright, we possess a representative of whom we are justly proud, irrespective of party considerations ; the mighty champion of those principles which he considers to be identified with peace, law, order, truth, progress, and liberty—of lofty and commanding genius—orator, statesman, patriot, gifted with rare excellence to persuade, to convince, to subdue, to delight, to command. When he speaks the Senate listens, and the swift-winged lightning waits to convey his words to great cities and distant lands ; a veritable hammer in controversy ; sometimes exalted to high position ; who has never been known to pervert his glorious gifts for any ignoble or unworthy purposes, for selfish ambition, or place or power. Such men belong more to their country than to a party, and it is of them, by them, and through them that empires are governed and history is made."

Earl Granville and the Marquis of Hartington have held, and do deservedly hold high place in the estimation of Liberals ; the former nobleman is the recognised leader of the party in the Lords, and the latter in the Commons. They have rendered, and do render, great service to the cause they espouse, and they may fully be trusted to go forward in the front of the ranks in any contest in which Liberalism is engaged.

Q. Who are the leaders of the Tories to-day ?

A. They have *no leaders* — they have only a leader, the Earl of Beaconsfield, better known as Mr. Benjamin Disraeli—he is the chief embodiment of Toryism, and none of his followers dares dissent from his dictation. Minor satellites move around this great bubble, but when this bubble bursts, as burst it will, these satellites will curse the power that has held them in leash so long—the chief satellite is the Marquis of Salisbury, and he may be said to come nearest to Beaconsfield as a representative of the party.

Q. Are not the leading points of Earl Beaconsfield's career very suggestive ?

A. Very ! Uncertainty rests upon the day and the year of his birth ; equal uncertainty upon where he was born, whether in the capital or in Bucks ;* a life of more than seventy years compels the world to say " he is as *uncertain* as the wind to-day." His emergence from obscurity was as a writer of novels, and "Vivian Grey" was his first waif cast upon the stream.

---

* " Lord Beaconsfield," a Biography, by T. P. O'Connor, M.A.

In 1832, after the passing of the Reform Bill, he twice presented himself to the Electors of High Wycombe as a candidate, advocating extreme Radical opinions at both elections, and was defeated. In 1833 he paid his addresses to the Electors of Marylebone, with the same radical opinions, but was disappointed. In 1834 he again wooed High Wycombe, and was again rejected. Finding his *Radical* opinions not in favour, he tried the Electors of Taunton as a *Tory*, in 1835, and they would not have him. On the death of the King, in 1837, Maidstone chose him as its Tory Member; in 1841 he sat for Shrewsbury, and was arrested for debt on the hustings by the side of Col. Tomline; in 1847 he was chosen as the second member for Bucks, which he continued to represent until his elevation to the House of Lords. In 1848 he became the leader of the Tories in the House of Commons. His first Chancellorship of the Exchequer was in 1852, and in 1868, on the retirement of Lord Derby, he became Prime Minister of England. In 1876 (August) he was raised to the peerage as Lord Beaconsfield.

Q. What is Lord Beaconsfield's system of government—how has it been described by the " Times " ?

A. "As a system of audacity and chicane."*

Q. In what language has the " Times " described both the Tories and their leader, Lord Beaconsfield ?

A. "**The Tories follow a guide who habitually confuses the boundaries of truth and error.**"†

Q. How has Lord Beaconsfield been described in one of the leading reviews of the day ?‡

A. Thus: "Lord Beaconsfield is at his best when he is inconsistent. . . . Personal ambition is his sole motive, and he cares not how that ambition may be gratified. . . . There is a mire so black and so deep

---

* CHICANE—a shift, turn, or trick; sophistry, wrangling.—*Webster*.

† *Times*, July 30, 1868.   ‡ *North British Review*.

that no leader has a right to drag his followers through it. Through such a mire Lord Beaconsfield has dragged the country gentlemen of England. Under his guidance they have shrunk from no inconsistencies, they have stooped to any subterfuge which held out the faintest promise of temporary success. . . . . Sooner will the Ethiopian change his skin, and the leopard his spots, than Lord Beaconsfield relinquish a policy of intrigue."

Q. In what terms does Earl Beaconsfield's biographer* speak of him?

A. "I have proved, beyond a possibility of doubt in any reasonable mind, that throughout his whole career his sole absorbing thought has been himself, and that to carry out his own advancement he has sacrificed every principle which men hold dear ; I have proved that all through his life he has been playing with every feeling, with every public man, with every party, with every interest in England, with the recklessness of the foreigner to whom all these things were but as worthless cards in the great game of ambition he was playing." Referring to Mirabeau, and of some important redeeming points in his character, he goes on to say : "In Lord Beaconsfield I find no such redeeming feature ; that whole character is complete in its selfishness ; that whole career is uniform in its dishonesty ; there is, throughout, the same selfishness, calm, patient, unresting. Such a man the myriads of this mighty Empire accept as chief ruler ; to such a man it is given to control, by his single will, your fortunes and mine, and even those of countless generations yet to come. Which shall a near posterity most wonder at : the audacity of the impostor, or the blindness of the dupe?—the immensity of the worship, or the pettiness of the idol?"

Q. How do you describe the Marquis of Salisbury?

A. He is a Tory of the very oldest school; opposes every movement towards the people, and would

---

* "Lord Beaconsfield," a Biography, by T. P. O'Connor, M.A.

rather retrace the steps in the history of the country than hasten them onwards.

Q. What is the estimate these men have expressed of each other?

A. Of Lord Beaconsfield the Marquis said in the House of Commons, " You practically banish all honourable men from the political arena, and you will find in the long run that the time will come when your statesmen will become nothing but political adventurers; and that profession of opinions will be looked upon as so many political manœuvres for the purpose of attaining office. . . . I deeply regret the position of the Executive (Lord Beaconsfield's) should have been so degraded. I deeply regret to find the House of Commons has applauded a policy of legerdemain." *

Again he said, "I am utterly sceptical of their (Tories) power to restrain their erratic leader—he will have language of his own which he can quote in support of whatever policy he may feel disposed to adopt ; for it is part of his political skill to be able to refer to phrases of his own in favour of any course he may deem it advisable to take. He whispers to hon-gentlemen, 'Vote for me ; I am educating my party, and the moment the process is complete, all your wishes will be fulfilled.' I do not pretend to predict the probable course of the right hon. gentleman at the head of the Government. I should as soon undertake to tell you which way the weather-cock would point to-morrow."†

Q. What is Lord Beaconsfield's opinion of the Marquis of Salisbury?

A. He describes him as " a great master of gibes, and flouts, and jeers—he is not a man who measures his phrases."‡

---

* Hansard's Parliamentary Reports.
† Hansard's Parliamentary Reports.   ‡ Ibid, vol. 221, col. 1353.

Q. In the arena of Morals what words best describe the character of Lord Beaconsfield's Cabinet ?

A. The words of the *Times* : it is a Cabinet "that habitually confuses the boundaries of truth and error."

Q. How can you possibly substantiate such a charge ?
A. Falsehood is of three kinds :

    I. Falsehood in practice.
    II. Falsehood direct.
    III. Falsehood by evasion of the truth, the *suppressio veri*, or what is often termed "white lies."

I will give examples—as many more exist as the reader can possibly desire.

At Berlin Lord Beaconsfield met the members of Congress ostensibly aiming to carry out a certain policy in unity with them ; at that very time he had signed a secret treaty with Russia in direct opposition to the course he seemingly advocated in the Congress—that was practical falsehood in great activity.*

Falsehood direct was uttered by the Chancellor of the Exchequer in the House of Commons on the last night prior to the rising of the House for the Easter vacation in 1879, when he said, in answer to a question put to him, "There was no change whatever in our Indian policy " ;† at that moment the papers were preparing to announce the next morning a complete change, and to state that an order had been given for the dispatch of 7,000 troops to Europe to take part, if need be, in the settlement of the Eastern Question, and 30,000 others were to be held in readiness to take the same route if the exigencies of war rendered it necessary—this denial was undoubtedly made in the full knowledge that it was contrary to fact.

Wilful falsehood by evasion is illustrated by another leading member of the Cabinet publicly stating in the

---

* See Clayden's " England Under Lord Beaconsfield," pp. 414-422.
† Hansard's Parliamentary Reports, vol. 239, cols. 1391-2.

House of Lords, when Mr. Marvin's extraordinary reve-
lation of the secret treaty was made, "that there was
no truth in the statement, that there was no authority
for it," and then subsequently acknowledging "that
the terms of the treaty as revealed were substantially
true, but they were published without authority."*

Evasive and untrue statements, undoubtedly many,
if not all of them, wilfully so, lie so thick all over the
floor of the ministerial side of the House that Mr.
Cross, a leading member of the Cabinet, felt con-
strained to say, "There is a lying spirit abroad."†

*Q. What has the country gained from six years of
Tory rule?*

A. Examine for yourself—take its home policy.
Six sessions have gone, and there is no act passed in
the whole six having within its scope any points of
value to the nation as a whole—can you name one?
I cannot—no beneficial act that marks the period of
Lord Beaconsfield's rule. He has burked, meddled
or muddled over the few things he has attempted,
and the six years have been, like the Premier himself,
barren of a single offspring to bear his title for good
for all time to come.

Take his financial arrangements. Here he has
thrown them into confusion worse confounded; con-
verted large surpluses into very large deficits; found
the income tax at 2d., has raised it to 5d., and
prepares us in the next budget for an increase to 8d.
or 9d., if not more, to meet his war expenditure;
increasing taxation, he lives like a spendthrift on
"promises to pay," till the effect upon the industry
of the country is such that the distress of the working
classes is greater to-day than it has been for the last
thirty years.

Look at his foreign policy—east, west, north, and
south—and where is there to be seen one ray of light
to compensate for the enormous waste of blood and
treasure shed and thrown into eternity in carrying

---

* Hansard, vol. 240, cols. 1060-1.   † Hansard, vol. 237.

out the most unjust and unrighteous wars ever undertaken by this nation? The stormy petrel of the House of Commons, Lord Beaconsfield has proved himself the stormy petrel of the nation as Premier; from an annual expenditure of £71,000,000 on taking office he has led the nation on to £85,000,000 a year, and is still increasing it. We shall soon have thrust on our shoulders the burden of paying for the Government of India, as it is impossible to raise in that part of the world an income anywhere near the costs of Government as now being developed; we may, therefore, look forward to find at a very early day the expenditure of the country raised to £100,000,000 a year, unless prevented by the Electors.

Q. And for all this, what has he accomplished by his foreign policy?

A. He pledged himself to " maintain the integrity of Turkey," and encouraged that power in its opposition to the will of Europe, but cowardly stood aside and refused to draw the sword when that integrity was torn to shreds : he had the opportunity to maintain the glory of England as the friend of oppressed nationalities and the defender of the helpless against their bloodthirsty tyrants, but his Government threw the oppressed overboard, and supported the oppressor against the Christian peoples of the East. He claims to have frustrated the schemes of Russia, but he has been the unconscious cat's-paw by which Russia has drawn and is drawing her chestnuts out of the fire ; and now the newly-constituted governments of Eastern Europe, instead of looking to England as their deliverer, regard England with suspicion and gratefully hold out their hands to Russia.

Q. What has he accomplished in South Africa?

A. The slaughter of many thousands of a brave people fighting for their hearths and homes in their own territory, because that territory was coveted by the white man as was Naboth's vineyard by Ahab ;

the cause of quarrel, "Cetewayo, the Zulu King, must no longer keep his soldiers celibates, but must give them permission to marry at will, and he must consent to reduce the number of his standing army ; " and to-day, though nominally the conquerors, we have inherited a legacy of trouble, and disorder, and chronic rebellion that is likely to tell its tale upon English finances for many years to come.

Q. What has the Tory Government accomplished in Afghanistan ?

A. It has broken up the strongest government that the country had had for many years, and confusion, anarchy, the ravages of war, and desperation prevail in its stead.   Here, again, is a people fighting in defence of their native land against invaders.   Treated as rebels, though they owe us no allegiance, they are strung up to the gallows by scores ; rapine, destruction, cruelty rampant ; justice, mercy, compassion having no place in the councils of the authorities ; burning and sacking of villages, turning children, women, the aged out of their homes into the fierce cold of an Afghan winter, and then burning and destroying their houses and their winter stores of food before their eyes—this is the course pursued by "a truly Christian Government," that Government scrupulously and studiously preventing the truth from coming home to the English reader by gagging the press, and by transmitting only such information as it pleases, and which, like most of its acts and statements, often proving unworthy of credit.

Q. Have our arms increased in military prestige during the last six years ?

A. No ; rather the contrary ; we have been fighting with savages in the south, with semi-savages in the east, and, with all our power and splendid arms, in more than one engagement we have been worsted, our honour sullied, and although in the end we have proved the stronger, that has arisen from our arms of precision and their more deadly power rather than from superior courage or more elaborate skill.

Q. If war had been in Europe, and we were in battle array against a great European power, what might have happened ?

A. For my country's honour I forbear to express an opinion ; let the reader think it out for himself; the military episodes of the last three years give a gloomy answer.

Q. Looking at the enormous increase in the costs of Government under Tory rule, I ask, is the payment of taxes beneficial or prejudicial to the people ?

A. Prejudicial. Though Governments cannot be maintained without cost, and taxation to maintain good Government is a necessity, yet every penny required to carry on war policy not absolutely demanded by the people is unjust and illegitimate. The Zulu war was commenced without the first sanction of Parliament, and so was the Afghan. Lord Salisbury's instructions to Lord Lytton were " Find cause of quarrel with Shere Ali, the Ameer of Afghanistan, and if you cannot find a cause, make one." No legitimate cause was found, and Lord Lytton made one. Parliament was called upon to ratify accomplished facts and to pay, but was not first asked to sanction them ere they were begun ; and, in accordance with true constitutional principles, the payment of taxes for these wars is unjust.

Every shilling taken in taxation is unproductive, is an injury to the wage-winner, and is so much loss to the national resources ; every working man earning twenty shillings weekly, and paying, say, three shillings in taxes, is no better off than if he had earned seventeen shillings ; could he have his twenty shillings in full he would be at liberty to spend three shillings more weekly on himself and his family, and would be so much better off, financially ; **increased taxation**

means increased burdens upon the masses and less money
to spend by those who win it; a Government, therefore, that unjustly increases taxation is a guilty
Government, doing irreparable injury to the whole
community.

Q. What are the prospects of England to-day?

A. As regards the Monarchy, I see "a cloud no
bigger than a man's hand rising up out of the sea."

Q. What is its aspect?

A. Threatening—There are various factors at work
at high pressure tending to produce inimical results.
Of these, two stand out prominently, and more and
more force their operations upon public attention ;
they are—

    I. The assumption of Imperial power by and
       on behalf of the Crown against the consent
       of the people.

    II. The retirement into PRIVATE life of the
       Sovereign of these realms.

Q. Will you explain your meaning?

A. I will : The purchase of the Suez Canal shares
at a cost of several millions of the public funds at
the will of the Minister, without consulting Parliament
until the fact was accomplished, contrary to the
ordinary constitutional practice of the country, is
Imperialism.

The deportation of native Indian troops to Europe
to fight the battles of England without the sanction of
Parliament, thus becoming a standing menace to
European powers, and to our domestic liberties,
thereby showing the power of the Crown in troublous
times, should they arise, to deport again to our foreign
arsenals these troops, so setting at liberty our
British born soldiers to be rapidly brought within the
limits of our own shores to overawe any opposition to
the will of the reigning powers in case of need, is
Imperialism.

By making and signing secret treaties involving

immense responsibilities upon England, in various parts of the world, without the knowledge or consent of Parliament, and then boldly calling upon it simply to ratify facts accomplished ; in these and many other ways practically asserting the power of the Crown to be greater than the power of Parliament, manifestly increasing the prerogative of the monarch at the expense of the constitution, these are forces at work not favourable to existing institutions.

II. A sovereign to reign in the hearts of his subjects and to be popular must be seen, and must be frequently seen surrounded by all the splendour of the state he personifies ; a sovereign of whom the people only hear that last week he was in Balmoral ; this week he is at Osborne, and next month he will be at Windsor or on the Continent, and so continues to do for a long series of years, is not likely to retain strong hold upon the affections of the people, and especially so if he never take up his abode in his capital, or for only an hour or two to make private calls, who leaves his capital without a court or the vraisemblance of a court. Such a sovereign is familiarising the people with republican forms of government, and creating desire for their actual existence. "If the country can be satisfactorily governed by Parliament with the sovereign in retirement, then it can be governed equally well without the ornament of the crown," is the argument used by many persons to-day ; and it is on behalf of the reigning family, of the institutions under which we have lived so long, and on behalf of the heir-apparent we thus plainly utter these words of warning to those more intimately concerned therein.

Q. What is the present relative position of the principal European powers ?

A. Let the following statistics* testify. They show

Europe "armed" on "a peace-footing," with the costs of the same; also the numbers of the forces available in some States on "a war-footing;" while it is well to remind the reader that the whole of this enormous annual war expenditure is defrayed by taxation drawn from the pockets of the peoples themselves.

War Forces of Europe and their Cost "at Peace."

Countries.		Peace-footing.		War-footing.
Austria		267,332	... ...	800,000
Belgium		40,000	... ...	100,000
France		502,697	... ...	1,000,000
				(and more as required)
Germany		401,659	...	1,800,000
		(If necessary, Germany can place in the field 2½ millions of men, without drawing upon her last resources.)		
Great Britain { Army ...		135,625		
Navy ...		58,800		
India ...		62,653		
Italy		199,557	... ...	444,509
Netherlands		99,506		
Russia		765,872	... ...	1,213,259
Switzerland		202,397		
Spain		151,668		
Turkey		350,000		

Total on "peace-footing" 3,237,766 men set apart for purposes of war.

Annual Costs for Maintenance of the States of Europe on a "Peace-footing."

Austria						£10,674,260
Belgium...						1,642,520
France						23,317,654
Germany						20,501,797
Great Britain						32,213,000
Italy						9,890,991
Netherlands						256,724
Russia						29,680,238
Switzerland						586,237
Spain						5,930,000

Turkey has never presented any report of her National Income and Expenditure, but the costs for her Army and Navy may be reckoned safely at not less than 6,000,000

Total Annual Cost for "peace-footing" £140,693,421

Do not these statistics furnish the bitterest satire
it is possible to conceive of the term "peace-footing"?
and also on the " peaceful " (?) character of the
governments of Europe?   Bismarck, in Germany,
with its tremendous forces, yet fears the growing
strength of his neighbours, and, alarmed, he has just
hastened to the Reichstag for authority to add 62,000
additional troops to his army ; this must be followed
by his neighbours sooner or later, and so, burden on
burden, tax on tax, calamity on calamity are being
heaped on to the shoulders of longsuffering peoples,
until eventually the end must come ! And fearful will
that end be for many when it does appal the
world !

Let me ask the reader, for whom do these armies
exist and are these costs incurred ?   Do they benefit
the peoples of the nationalities of Europe ?   And if
the peoples of Europe, each in their nation, were polled
to-morrow on the question, " Shall the present
enormous military and naval arrangements be per-
petuated ? " would not an immense majority reply,
" No ! their existence, as now, is a disgrace to
humanity and to the reputed civilization of the
world !"

Jealous and suspicious of each other, the Governments of Europe are busily engaged in perfecting and
increasing their military systems and their weapons
of war at enormous cost of men and treasure.   France,
Germany, Austria, Italy, Turkey, Russia, and England
diplomatically striving which can most cunningly
outbid and overreach the other, which shall have the
strongest army, the best equipments, the most readiness to take the field, and when the day of battle comes,
as assuredly it will come (for all these preparations must
inevitably lead to strife) where will England be ? and
with whom will she be allied ?   Will she stand aloof,
or will she again reject Andrassy notes, send her
noble Marquis to new Congresses with one definite

object in view, and give her Ambassador in another quarter full power to thwart and upset the efforts of the Marquis? Will her Premier again betake himself to Berlin with smooth-faced professions, whilst at the same time he is signing secret treaties privately with single members of the Congress to upset what he is openly claiming to desire? **Who shall say? None but the Electors have the power to say, and it is to them the Nation looks for definite resistance to the policy pursued by Lord Beaconsfield.**

Q. What will be the probable condition of the people?

A. As long as the present Cabinet is in power so long trade will be depressed; taxation will be largely increased; bad times for the producer and the consumer will continue, and the whole tendency of the country will be downwards, morally and financially.

Q. Why should this be so?

A. Because a Tory Government is always willing for war; is unstable and uncertain in its policy, should it happen to have one, and people within the kingdom and the foreigner without never can say from month to month what a Tory Ministry will do; because the Ministry and the friends of the Ministry have always "their uncles, their cousins, and their wives' brothers-in-law" in want of solid salaries; because many of their octogenarian supporters are waiting for appointments of £2,000 a year and do nothing, and younger men readily consent to £1,200 a year for posts for the duties of which they have no knowledge; because a Tory Government always means public waste and great extravagance; curtailment of the rights and liberties of the people; gagging of the press; hatred of freedom and abhorrence of liberty; a love of absolutism and the excesses of despotic power.

Q. What is the battle-cry of the Liberals?
A. PEACE; RETRENCHMENT; REFORM.

Q. Can you explain this cry?

A. Readily. By Peace is meant the maintenance of terms of amity and concord with all peoples, small as well as great, wherein it can be maintained with honour ; creating no voluntary causes of quarrel, wasting no national finances on paltry, unjust, or unnecessary wars, but husbanding the nation's resources so that, if necessary at any time to strike for the honour or integrity of the Empire, then to strike with the requisite energy and force to be invincible. That is the meaning of this term Liberal policy gives.

Retrenchment, is keeping costs of government within the legitimate requirements and means of the nation ; the creation of no sinecures, perpetration of no "jobbery ;" resolutely bringing the expenditure within the estimates ; firmly making known the liabilities of the nation, whatever they may be ; and never attempting to hoodwink the people by corruptly dealing with the true state of the finances.

The Reform sought to be carried out is to remove anomalies ; to wipe away any blots still continued from past legislation ; to adopt means having for their object the better condition of the people, and to give to every man an interest in the wellbeing and security of the state—to improve whatever is improvable, and to remove whatever is objectionable and injurious to the body politic.

Q. What is the duty of Electors at the coming General Election?

A. Calmly to consider what the best interests of the nation righteously demand ; to listen to no Ministerial cajolery, to be caught by no "rise in chemicals," to be gulled by no "Liberal-Conservatives," but to be guided by a due sense of their responsibility in their voting, and to give their votes to the candidates of that great Liberal party which has proved itself the friend of the people, the defender of their rights and liberties, and the advocate of freedom throughout the world.

43

Q. Why should they do this?

A. Because a *Liberal Government reduces* the public charge ; keeps the departments *within* the estimates ; *diminishes* the taxation of the country ; and *reduces* the National Debt ; maintains the *just* honour and integrity of the Empire ; defends the freedom of the press and of the subject ; and is ever ready to assist in delivering oppressed nationalities from the power of the oppressors ; whilst a *Tory* Government *increases* the public charge ; allows the departments to *spend more* than the estimates, thus creating deficits ; creates places and salaries for its supporters ; gags the press ; and attempts to set aside at will the great principles of the constitution under which we live.

Q. Should the present Government be trusted now ?

A. No! a thousand times, No! It has signally failed in domestic legislation through the whole term of its tenure of office ; it has meddled in Eastern affairs only to muddle them ; its efforts to curb Russia have resulted in Russia obtaining that for which she fought, and it has succeeded in making that country our deadly enemy ; it has burdened the nation with increased taxation to such an extent that the resources of the people must feel the baneful effects for many years to come ; in short, to quote the words of a recent writer, " The Government is a bankrupt Government, living like a capitalist with no visible source of income ; governing with no recognized principles and no certain policy ; led by Lord Beaconsfield, who is a phenomenon in politics of the same order as Leotard and Blondin on a less illustrious stage. They have a great establishment infinitely beyond their means, and they mean to keep it up if they can raise the wind. To do this is, therefore, the work and duty of the hour. Steal the Reform kite, and fly it ; and if it fail, send up ' No Popery ;' and where ' No Popery ' fails to answer, let it be ' Throne, Church, and Constitution ' ; will claim to be Liberal-

Conservatives for the hour to deceive the undecided Liberal, and then betray him ; and, where these fail, will then stoop to the lowest depths of Democracy itself. Lord Beaconsfield and his followers will be all things to all men if by any means they can catch some. Anything on earth to raise the wind."

Electors of Great Britain, be warned in time. Let no man deceive you by cunning craft or deceptive smiles ; carefully consider the facts and principles contained in these pages, and the facts and incidents that have occurred during the last twenty years, and are occurring to-day, and then I have no fear as to the way in which your reason and your interest will counsel you to vote at the coming General Election.

TO AUTHORS.

HOW TO PUBLISH, AND ON THE EASIEST TERMS.

Messrs. KERBY & ENDEAN'S

Large experience and personal practical knowledge of everything connected with the production of books, from setting the first type to placing the complete book in the hands of the public, are sufficient guarantee that all that can be done to render books successful will be done by them, and they place their services at the command of authors about to publish. They undertake commissions for every class of publication—Religious, Scientific, Political, Educational, &c.

SERMONS AND PAMPHLETS

Produced at the Shortest Notice, and in the Best Style.

KERBY & ENDEAN'S NEW BOOKS.

In 1 handsome vol., 4to, beautifully illustrated, 6s.,

WILLIAM PIGG, Esq., M.P., AND HIS AD-
VENTURES in HAM(P)SHIRE. Illustrated by the Hon. Charlotte Ellis.
The humorous narrative by the Rev. H. A. MARTIN, of Laxton.

This is a witty burlesque of life; with a General Election in prospect,
Mr. Pigg will be a great favourite.

"There is a fresh and original humour about the whole work."—*Times.*

"We can safely recommend this book, for the young, or for the drawing-room
table—there is much originality skilfully developed—we have laughed heartily over
it."—*Freemason*

"The drawings are clever, reproduced with considerable breadth and power."—
Live Stock Journal.

"Exceedingly diverting—exceptionally clever drawings—originality of style, rich
though quiet humour, which cannot fail to be greatly appreciated." *Court Journal.*

THE MARVELLOUS LITTLE HOUSE-
KEEPERS: What They Did, and How They Did It. By IDA JOSCELYNE.
Illustrated. Fcap 8vo, 2s. 6d. This is an admirable book for all readers, full
of sound, practical information, most pleasantly given.

"In the form of a story the author gives valuable hints, suggestions and recipes
to young people—is a capital book for girls."—*Court Journal.*

"We can most sincerely recommend this work to the notice of our younger and
our elder readers—we can conscientiously assert we have seldom met with any which
has commended itself more to our approval."—*Freemason.*

THE STEPPING STONES: An Allegory. By
the Author of "Flower and Fruit," &c. Royal 16mo, Frontispiece, cloth, 2s.

"This most pleasant little book we can most earnestly commend to the notice of
those seeking books for the young,—its language is lucid, ideas elevated, and its
moral good in every sense."—*Freemason.*

The Best Cookery Books of the Day.

BREAKFASTS and LUNCHEONS at HOME.
By SHORT, Author of "Dinners at Home." Crown 8vo, cloth, 2s. 6d.

"This little book supplies a want frequently felt by housekeepers. There is
variety enough to suit all palates ; clear and simple enough for all to understand."—
Dublin Evening Mail.

"We commend it earnestly to all those good house-wives who wish to preserve
health and to make their home and their husbands comfortable."—*See Reviews.*

LA FONTAINE'S FABLES (Books I. and II.),
and VICTOR HUGO'S ORIENTALES (Book I.). English Translation, by
J. N. FAZAKERLEY, side by side with the original. Crown 8vo, cloth limp, 1s. 6d.

"A literal and yet idiomatic translation of La Fontaine's verse in the English
rendering, and the difficulties in so rendering have been overcome."—*Examiner.*

KERBY & ENDEAN'S NEW BOOKS.

DINNERS at HOME: How to Order, Cook,
and Serve them. By SHORT. Fourth Edition. Crown 8vo, handsomely
bound, 5s.

"Dainty and highly satisfactory recipes."—"Really excellent."—"Appetising
volume."—"Recipes excellent."—"Menus most useful."—*See Reviews.*

"The dainty and highly satisfactory recipes in these pages will be welcome in
most households. A large choice given: 'Savoury dishes' and 'Sweets' will tempt
the reader to try the skill of his cook without loss of time. Short's 'Hints' will make
every cook wiser and better who will exactly follow her instructions."—*Pall Mall
Gazette.*

"*Recipes* excellent, and *menus* most useful."—*Liverpool Albion.*

"*What is chiefly to be admired in it is* its *eminently practical character,* full of
common sense and valuable information."—*Irish Times.*

"A cookery book admirably arranged for mistresses to provide good dinners IN AN
ECONOMICAL MANNER. *Specially designed to give the mistress* of the household
such *information as will enable her,* without constant attendance in the kitchen,
to have a thoroughly satisfactory dinner served at home. Excellent hints. Every
lady with this book ought to provide an excellent dinner."—*Western Daily
Mercury.*

"A large variety of recipes for each course from soups to dessert—several dishes
not in ordinary books of *cuisine* elaborately detailed."—*Belfast News Letter.*

MIECISLAS: A Study from Life. From the
Original by T. LOUIS OXLEY. Demy 8vo, paper, 2s.; cloth, 3s.

"It is the misery of dogmatism that it wishes to teach what only life can do."—
Auerbach.

LE FILS NATUREL: A Play in Five Acts.
By ALEXANDRE DUMAS, Fils. Translated from the Original by T. LOUIS
OXLEY, Author of "From Calais to Karlsbad." Crown 8vo, cloth, 5s.

YADASTÉ (The Wager). An Original Comedy
in One Act. By MIECISLAS KAMIENSKI. Translated and adapted to the
English Stage by T. LOUIS OXLEY. Crown 8vo, 1s.

WHAT IS THE ETERNAL HOPE OF CANON
FARRAR? Are not its Doctrines Morally and Spiritually Dangerous? Also a
Correspondence with the Canon, by J. RUSSELL ENDEAN, Author of "Lending
unto the Lord." Crown 8vo, cloth, 2s. 6d.

"A very interesting religious controversial work, which criticises in a scholarly
style 'Eternal Hope,' by Canon Farrar. Evidently Mr Endean came off triumph-
ant."—*Cork Examiner.*

"Mr Endean's criticism and accompanying correspondence are well worth reading
and specially interesting to students of matters theological."—*Western Mercury.*

"Deeply interesting subject—this book is a sharp, business-like *brochure,* in which
he drives the Canon hard, and his arguments are worth reading."—*Fountain.*

"Mr Endean's refutation is characterised by singular ability."—*Court Journal.*

"Its arguments are directed with great earnestness and considerable force against
the positions of Canon Farrar."—*Homilist.*

"Is an attempt to expose and upset the reasoning and rhetoric of the Westminster
preacher. Mr Endean writes with sharpness and point; catching up the Canon with
much adroitness."—*Christian World.*

www.ingramcontent.com/pod-product-compliance
Lightning Source LLC
Chambersburg PA
CBHW032134080426
42733CB00008B/1070